_____

From:

_____

MY BESTIE,

You Were...

A celebration of you
and your awesomely one-of-a-kind YOU-ness!

you were

something sparkly,

you'd be

_____

_____ .

you were

a fancy drink,

you'd be

_____ .

you were

a dream vacation spot,

you'd be

_____ .

you were

a fairy tale character,

you'd be

_____

because

_____.

you were a fragrance,

you'd smell like

_____

&

_____.

you were

a baked goodie,

you'd be

_____

because

_____.

you were

a classic album,

you'd be

_____.

you were

a holiday decoration,

you'd be

_____.

you were

a feel-good movie

or binge-worthy show,

you'd be

_____.

you were

something with wheels,

you'd be

_____!

you were

a toy or game,

you'd be

_____

because

_____ .

you ran the world,

there would be more

_____

and less

_____.

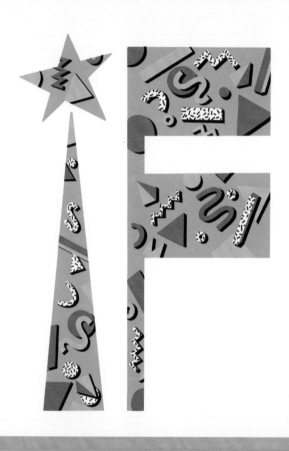

you were

a piece of good

(or bad!) advice,

you'd be

"_____

_____."

you were

a baby animal

doing something cute

in a YouTube™ video,

you'd be

_____

_____ .

you were

a tree or plant,

you'd be

_____.

you were

something homemade,

you'd be

_____.

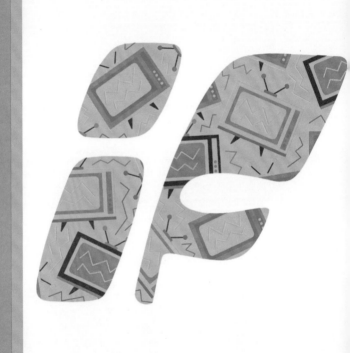

they made a movie

about us,

_____

&

_____

could totally star as

you and me.

you were

_____

for Halloween,

I'd 100% be

_____ .

you took

a time machine to

_____,

you'd blow their minds

with your

_____ !

you were a band,

you'd be

_____.

you were an emoji,

you'd be

_____

(and maybe

_____).

you and I

were together

in a past life,

I bet we were

_____.

you were

a sitcom character,

your catchphrase

would be

"_____

_____."

you were a wizard,

you'd use your powers to

_____

and

_____!

you were

a retro fashion,

you'd be

_____.

you were

a star,

you'd be famous for

_____.

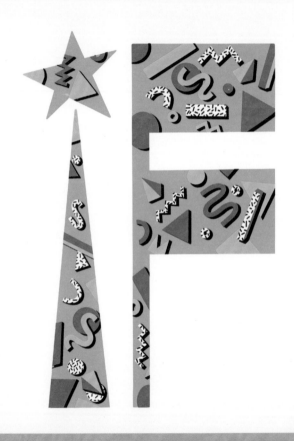

you were

an amusement park ride,

you'd be

_____.

we had

a secret clubhouse,

it'd be

_____

and located in

_____ .

and when

we're super old and

_____,

let's make a plan to

_____.

you weren't my

_____,

life would be

a whole lot less

_____!

Wherever you go

and whatever

you want to do, try,

or become...

you're
the best!

Created, published, and distributed by Knock Knock
6695 Green Valley Circle, #5167
Culver City, CA 90230
knockknockstuff.com
Knock Knock is a registered trademark of Knock Knock LLC

ISBN: 978-168349434-8
UPC: 825703-50312-8

10 9 8 7 6 5 4 3 2 1